# Shapes!

by Chris MacCaulay

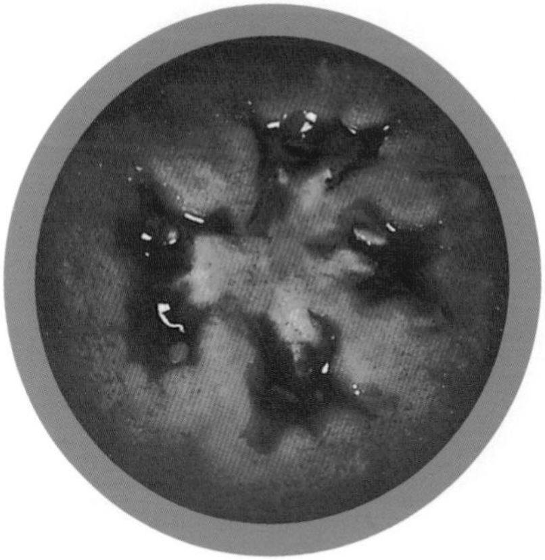

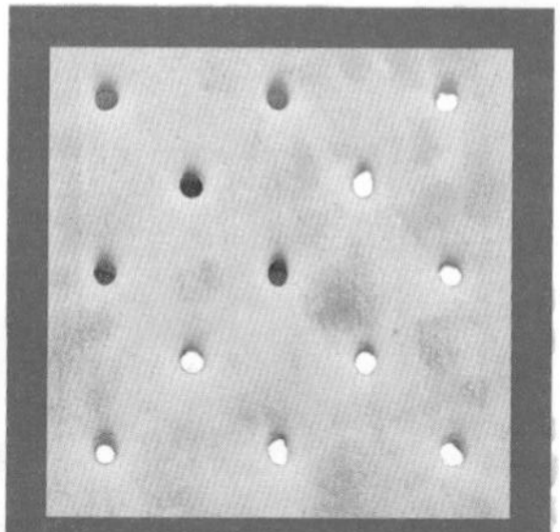

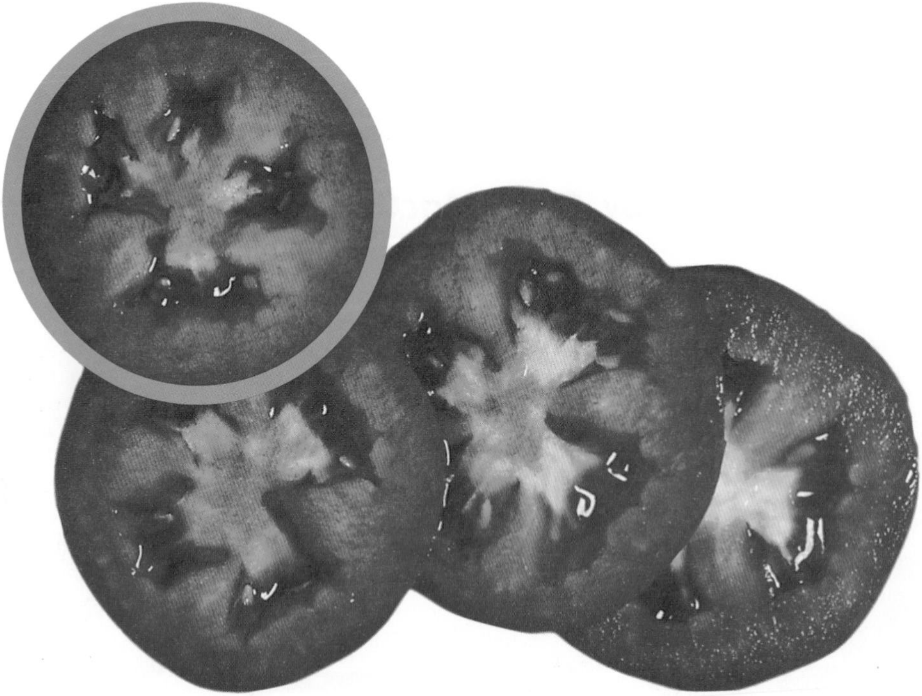

I like .
tomatoes

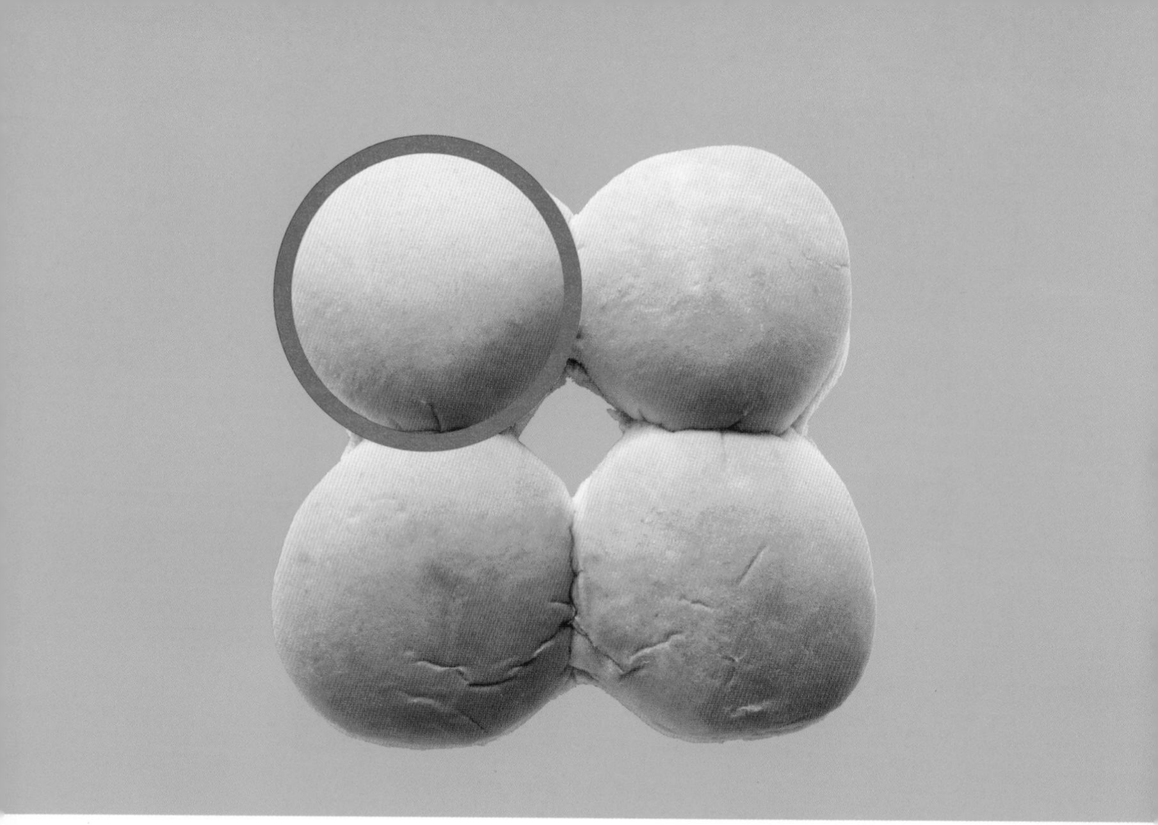

I like  .

**buns**

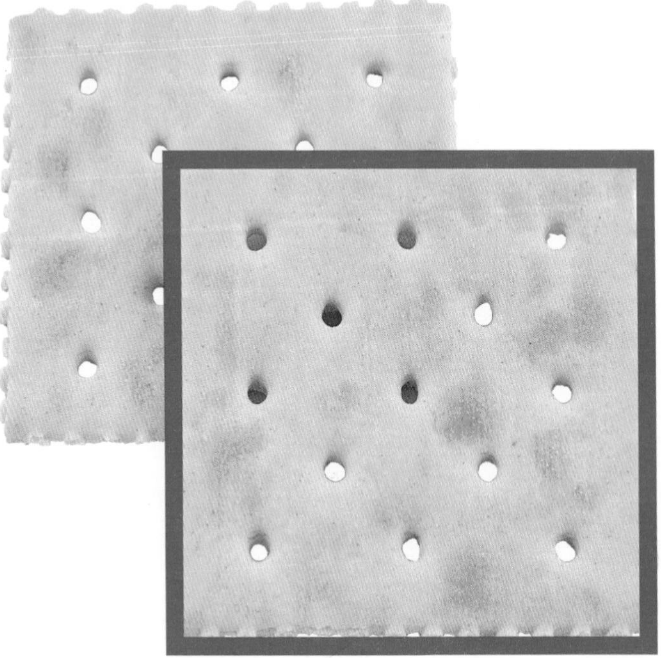

I like  .

crackers

(l)The McGraw-Hill Companies, Inc./Jacques Cornell photographer, (r)James Jackson/Dorling Kindersley/Getty Images

I like  .
bread

I like .

sandwiches

I like  .

pizza

I like  .
cheese

FoodCollection/age fotostock